DEFINE YOUR DESTINY

A SELF-AWARENESS JOURNEY TOWARD SERVANT LEADERSHIP

KELVIN A. REDD

ISBN: 1500501182
ISBN 13: 9781500501181
Library of Congress Control Number: 2014912606
CreateSpace Independent Publishing Platform
North Charleston, South Carolina

DEDICATION

To all the servant leaders who have helped me along my journey.

TABLE OF CONTENTS

FOREWORD

Kelvin Redd is a brilliant structural, empathic thinker who embodies passion and focus. As an Emergenetics workshop presenter, participants give him kudos on his sincerity and enthusiasm. He represents our company with high quality and integrity. He is an implementer who fuses information with care, verve, thoughtfulness, and grace…a perfect example of a servant leader.

Reading this book will be like being a student in one of his workshops. It will help you define your desires, vision, future education, self-awareness, relationships, and good health. Each section is rich with valuable information reinforced with life stories, personal reflections, and self-assessment questions to ponder.

Kelvin's commitment to making a difference in people's lives and his desire to build a servant leadership community is a testament for his love for others. His stories tell who he is and not what he thinks he should be. I believe his observations will be useful for your own learning and personal development.

Geil Browning, PhD
CEO/Founder
Emergenetics International

ACKNOWLEDGMENTS

To Kristina and Kirsten Redd, I love you both dearly. To my parents, James and Marie Redd, thank you for being there for me. I would not be where I am without you. To my sister, Krystal, I am still your biggest fan. To my nephew, Tramarius, I hope I can make you proud. To my Aunt Bernice, Aunt Jerri, Uncle Joe, and Cousin Joann, when I was down, you were there for me. To Fran and my Pastoral Institute coworkers, thank you for your support and encouragement. To Sherrie Gilbert, Mike Jones, and Matt Gillespie, each of you was heaven sent. To Heidi Newman, thank you for making *Define Your Destiny: A Self-Awareness Journey Toward Servant Leadership* a reality. Finally, to Mr. Bill Turner, thank you for your vision, for our comforting and enlightening talks, and for providing me with the opportunity to be the Director of the Center for Servant Leadership.

INTRODUCTION

Self-awareness is the most important characteristic of a servant leader. The Center for Servant Leadership, a division of the Pastoral institute, defines servant leadership as a lifelong journey that includes the discovery of one's self, a desire to serve others and a commitment to lead. *Define Your Destiny: A Self-Awareness Journey Toward Servant Leadership* is my pilgrimage to self-awareness. Through personal stories, examples, observations, and experiences, my hope is that this manuscript will assist you in defining your own destiny.

As a result, there are three distinct reasons why I believe I am more than capable of showing you how to mold your destiny. First, when I began my college career at Auburn University, a lot people asked me what I was going to study. I had always had a keen interest in the biographies of historical figures. Ultimately, I decided to major in history. All of these years later I am still asked why. For me, the answer is quite simple. I wanted to know what makes great people great.

Second, when I was growing up, for fourteen years, my father, James B. Redd, was the head basketball coach at Central High School in Phenix City, Alabama. He was not an average coach. In fact, he was outstanding in just about everything he did. He won nearly 400 games and fifty of his players received college scholarships during that short time period. He was valedictorian of his high school class and he majored in chemistry at Alabama State University in Montgomery, Alabama, where he graduated salutatorian. Later, Dad would become one of three of the first African-American teachers to work at Central High School. He was our town's lone chemistry and physics teacher until he retired in 1989. I learned a great deal from him, and many of the lessons he taught me are noted throughout this book.

Third, for thirteen years of my professional career I worked for Synovus Financial Corp. in Columbus, Georgia, a company voted by *Fortune* magazine in 1999 as the Best Place to Work in America. When you work for a *Best Place to Work* organization, you learn one of life's most simple truths: the value of taking care of people. I once heard Bill Turner, founding member of the Pastoral Institute and Board Member Emeritus of Synovus, say, "If you take care of the people, the profits will take care of themselves." In essence, that is the foundation of the philosophy of servant leadership.

Before we proceed, I would like for you to repeat to yourself: "I AM READY! I WAS BORN READY! I CAN DO GREAT THINGS WITH MY LIFE!" Now, let's get started.

CHAPTER 1

DEFINING DESIRE

In 1937, Napoleon Hill wrote what would eventually become one of the bestselling books of all time, *Think and Grow Rich*. The text came about after a meeting Hill had with legendary steel baron Andrew Carnegie. Hill says Carnegie wanted him to interview the leading men of his day in various industries to find out what made them successful. Carnegie wanted a success philosophy so that the "man on the street" could understand it. After numerous interviews and meetings with the leading achievers of his day, Hill concluded that they all had one thing in common: an understanding that 'desire' is step one to all achievement—"not a wish, not a want, but a keen, pulsating desire."[1]

I once heard a Harvard professor say, "Anyone can be successful. You can lie your way to success. You can steal your way to success. You can also cheat your way to success, but you cannot

---

[1] Napoleon Hill, *Think and Grow Rich* (New York: Fawcett Crest, 1960).

do that with greatness." Greatness transcends. I have always had a strong yearning to be prodigious—to be on stage, doing what I do best, which is speak. Once, while participating in a leadership retreat at Synovus, a co-worker of mine said, "Kelvin needs a stage." She was right. I needed to be seen and heard. I once wrote and starred in my own play in elementary school. It was that same drive that later served me when I ran for class office, on three different occasions, and won. I know what I just said sounds "me-focused" but that is far from my intent. I want to be as transparent with you as possible. Any desires that I have or have had are with the express purpose of utilizing my God-given talents to serve others. That is how strongly I feel about my calling and the work I do.

My dream-of-dreams has always been to travel the world to motivate people to be the best they can be by doing what they were put on this earth to do. Public speaking is where my talents lie. It runs in my family. My sister is a schoolteacher and a dynamic minister. One of the best speeches I have ever witnessed came from my oldest daughter, Kristina, when she gave a youth day speech at church. Of course, I am biased, but it was exceptional. However, it all starts with the patriarch of the family, my father.

During the early years of his career, Dad was often asked to speak at churches in and around town. Dad spoke with conviction, emotion, and POWER! To this day, I strongly believe he rivals some of the greatest orators of all time. People used to say he should have been a preacher. Of course, where I come from, that is what they have always said when someone expresses himself or herself in a highly intellectual manner. Dad probably could have been a minister: he was a voracious reader who knew the Bible quite well.

An early snapshot of my dad practicing a speech. He is still one of the greatest orators I've ever heard.

Although I did not know it at the time, this is where I learned how to speak publicly. I was probably seven or eight years old when Dad practiced his orations in my parents' bedroom with the door closed. His rhythmic voice reverberated throughout the house. I would sit outside the door and listen to his every word. Sometimes he would leave the door ajar, and I would see him rehearse. He was serious and his intensity was amazing.

Dad liked to listen to other speakers, too. That is where I got it from. My earliest memory of doing the same thing came when I was in the fifth grade. The high school football coach loaned Dad a motivational tape series with speeches made by several of the best college football coaches of the 1970s. When Dad was at basketball practice, I would sneak and listen to them. The boxed set included recordings from such men as Lou Holtz of Notre Dame, Bo Schembechler of Michigan, Tom Osborne of Nebraska, and Vince Dooley of Georgia. Dooley's speech was titled, "The Will to Prepare."

Years later, when I was the assistant director of the Center for Servant Leadership, I called Coach Dooley's office. I wanted to get a copy of that tape. His secretary answered the phone. I told her the story of how, as a little boy, I listened to the cassette tape of Coach Dooley speaking. I asked if I could get a copy. She told me to hold on for a moment while she checked with him. When she returned to the phone, she was laughing. She said that Coach Dooley was tickled because he had not thought of that cassette in a long time, but he would be glad to send me a copy. A week later, it arrived in the mail. I was thrilled, but the story does not end there. Not long afterward, he was a guest speaker at the Columbus Downtown Rotary Club, where I happened to be in the audience. I was fortunate to meet Coach Dooley that day, and I reminded him of our earlier exchange. It was great to have the opportunity to not only talk to him but thank him personally for sending me a copy of the tape.

My first meaningful experience connecting with an audience occurred when I was in the seventh grade and decided to run for class president. Even then I knew the ability to express myself in front of my peers would make me a viable candidate, but that was not going to be enough. I needed substance. Why did I want to be the student leader of my class? What did my classmates want? How could I get the students and faculty to work together to make our class the best ever? These were just a few of the questions I asked myself and my friends during the information-gathering stage. It was the knowledge that I gained about the needs of the students, not just my communications skills that won me the election.

I ran for class president again in the ninth grade. However, this time around, I asked my dad if he would write my campaign speech for me. He refused. He said it was the speaker's responsibility to put his own thoughts on paper. At first, I was miffed, but he knew what he was doing. Dad was forcing me to think on my own, which is the essence of being a good communicator. As a result, I won the election.

During my senior year, the local cable station began a news program for area high schools. The commentators would be the students themselves. Auditions were held after school. I wanted to be the sports director, but when I began reading my script, our coordinator jumped out of his seat and yelled, "You're it. You're going to be my anchor." I was a little disappointed. I thought I would be a natural doing the sports, but in the end, things turned out well, and it was an enjoyable experience for me.

My passion for speaking did not always get me what I wanted. Around the time of my high school graduation, I was expecting to be one of the speakers at the Class Night ceremony—our version of Baccalaureate. After all, I had twice been elected class president and once, vice president. However, one of the class sponsors chose another student. I was crushed and basically went through the entire service in a daze.

During my last semester of college, I needed only 18 hours to graduate, so I took a three-hour communications course. I thought it was going to be a piece of cake. How hard could it be? Wasn't speaking my forte? WRONG! This turned out to be one of the most difficult classes of my college career and it was not because of the curriculum.

My time at Auburn University was priceless, and I always enjoy going back.

At the outset, we were told that each student would have to present nine speeches over an eleven-week period. That seemed simple enough. I stood at the podium for seven straight assignments and gave what I thought were presentations that would make Dr. Martin Luther King, Jr. himself proud. I was factual. I told jokes, and students loved me. My grades, on the other hand, did not mirror my enthusiasm, or that of the students, as each week I received either a C or a D. I was dumbfounded. *Obviously, the teacher did not like me,* I thought to myself. To make matters worse, I failed the mid-term exam, which dropped my grade so low that I had an F average going into the final three weeks of the class.

On the eve of my ninth class, I was sitting in my apartment doing a lot of soul searching, and then it hit me. The number one rule of communication is: know your audience. Whenever I stood before my classmates, I was targeting them. I wanted to amaze the students with facts and humor. But *they* were not my audience. My audience was the professor.

From that point forward, I aimed everything I did at the instructor. I asked myself some powerful questions. For instance, who is he? What was his background? The answer: he was somewhat conservative and in his early 60s, and he never once smiled when I was at the lectern. The next time I stood before the class, I mirrored his behavior. I was conservative. I was matter-of-fact and to the point, and there was no humor. I will never forget the look on his face when I finished talking. He rose from his desk, clapped his hands and with a big smile on his face, he said, "Wasn't Kelvin just wonderful?"

I was on cloud nine. I learned a lot from that experience. My biggest lesson: Even when a room is filled with people, the audience may very well consist of one person.

Upon graduating from college, I began working as a management associate at Total System Services, Inc. in Columbus, Georgia. At the time, Total System was a subsidiary of Synovus Financial Corp. Both companies took pride in providing impeccable service to its clients and the community. Total System often brought in people to speak to the employees, so early on I was exposed to some exceptional facilitators.

Redd speaks at two area high schools

Redd

My community service activities at Synovus included speaking to area schools and civic organizations.

Eventually, I moved to Columbus Bank and Trust Company. Perhaps no other corporation in town was more community-oriented. The employees were encouraged to seek civic opportunities to serve in whatever capacity they felt comfortable. I told anyone who would listen to me that if there was a need for someone to speak to the area youth, I was their man. The prospect for me to assist in this capacity arose immensely.

When I became an underwriter, I went into the studio and recorded the audio version of this book, which at the time was titled *Define Your Destiny*. This amused many of my co-workers, which bothered me. It wasn't until several years later, after I had left the bank and became a certified Emergenetics Associate, that I would come to understand it was what a predominant right-brain thinker such as myself should expect from a prevailing left-brain environment.

Dr. Geil Browning has had a tremendous impact on my personal growth and development.

I had a life-altering experience when I was selected, along with thirteen co-workers, to participate in the Synovus Leadership Institute. We spent two weeks out of the year together, once in the spring and once in the fall, at a retreat center called Aberdeen Woods, just south of Atlanta.

We reported for our initial session on a Sunday evening, and it was at Aberdeen where I saw my first true workshop facilitator. I was awestruck by the way he led that first night. I remember sitting there and saying to myself, *I would love to do that.* Considering where I was at that point in my career, I never could have imagined that in less than a decade I would be one of the co-facilitators for the Synovus Leadership Institute. My desire to use my talents full-time had been sparked.

A Note to Parents: Make Sure It's Not *Your* Desire

Many parents vicariously live their lives through their children, which can be destructive if the adult encourages and coerces a child to pursue a certain sport, academic endeavor, or career. Sometimes the desires of the grownup are much stronger than those of the youngster.

When I was in middle school, I had a good friend named Jack. He was a year older than I and a couple of inches taller. We played a lot of basketball together in our back yards. One Sunday afternoon we were shooting hoops at his house. He was a good player, but I was beating him. When the game was almost over, Jack's father pulled his car into the driveway, got out and headed toward the front door. By the time he passed us, he heard me say, "game," which meant that I had won.

"He beat you?" Jack's dad asked in amazement.

"Yes, Sir," mumbled Jack, slowly putting his head down.

Jack's dad frowned as he walked into the house. This was a telling moment of things to come for a boy whom everybody felt had it "going on."

Jack played on the B-team when he was a sophomore in high school, and at end of the season, Dad called him up to the varsity when the squad made it to the state tournament. It was always a huge deal when a junior varsity player joined the "big boys." It was even bigger that year because the varsity was undefeated and ranked number one in the state. There was a perception among many that if a young kid played ball with the 11th and 12th graders, he was surely destined for a bright future. Of course, that is what other people thought. My dad did not think that way. If you wanted a spot on the team, irrespective of your class, you had to earn it. Jack did get a fair amount of playing time during his junior year, and he was a starter at the beginning of his senior season, playing ahead of a young man who was a grade-level below him. However, Jack's life changed forever one Friday night during a game early in the season when he sat on the bench for much of the second half.

"I believe Jack's dad is upset with me because he did not play much tonight," Dad said to my mother when we arrived home after the game.

Jack's dad usually congratulated my father after each game we won or offered words of encouragement if we lost (which was not very often). But he did not do it on that particular night. Dad thought it was a little unusual. Sure enough, he was right. Jack's father was more than a little upset. He was extremely angry.
The next day, on Saturday afternoon, the phone rang. It was Jack's dad. I could hear the conversation through the receiver because Jack's dad was talking loud.

"Well, if you do not want him to play on this team, make him quit," I heard my father say. The conversation lasted a few more minutes but that was it. Dad hung up the phone and said that Jack's father was angry because he did not play much the night before.

We had a game later that evening, but Jack did not show up. The following Monday morning, Jack's dad withdrew him from school.

It is important to note that Phenix City, Alabama, was and still is a relatively small town where everyone basically knows everyone else. Our basketball program was a perennial powerhouse. Most, if not all, of the boys on the team, had known each other through elementary and middle school. Word of Jack's father making him quit the team and withdrawing him from school was major news in the community.

What was my father's rationale for not playing Jack more on that particular Friday night? Someone on the team was playing better.

I witnessed a similar situation when I was in college. I had a friend, Sarah, who was an intelligent, nice and an outgoing sophomore, but she was miserable. One day I saw her in the Student Activities Center. She looked so sad. I asked her what was wrong. At first, Sarah would not say anything, but she finally broke down and told me her story. Her father was an engineer, and he wanted her to major in the same field. He thought it would be the perfect fit for her. Sarah did not want to study engineering. It was her desire to be a teacher but her father was insistent. Eventually, Sarah got up the courage to tell her father of her true desire. It was a cathartic conversation for both of them. Soon afterward, Sarah changed her major to education. From that point on, she seemed much happier.

It is not fair for a parent to force his child to live up to his own unfulfilled dreams. This type of behavior will shut down much-needed communication between the two. The juvenile may seek refuge from other people or in the form of other things like drugs and alcohol. Putting pressure on a young person to succeed in an endeavor that he may not even have the talent for, places a tremendous burden on him, and rest assured, it may be one that he will carry for a lifetime.

One of my heroes is retired General Colin Powell. During the early to mid-1990s, there was a groundswell of emotion on the part of many people in this country for him to run for the office of President of the United States. After all, how could the nation go wrong? General Powell was highly decorated. He was a Vietnam War veteran; he held a master's degree in business administration from George Washington University; he was Chairman of the Joint Chiefs of Staff; he appeared on the cover of *TIME* magazine as their Man of the Year. His book, *My American Journey*, was a bestseller. He was knighted by the Queen of England, and he had led the country through the Gulf War.

I remember watching General Powell on an episode of *20/20* as he was being interviewed by Barbara Walters. She wanted to know if he was going to seek the presidency, and she was persistent in her questioning. I will never forget General Powell's response: "I do not want to run for president. I do not have that 'burning in the belly.' I am a soldier." Wow! What fortitude and self-awareness. When just about every political poll in the country said he would win, General Powell knew himself well enough to say no. It was not his desire.

It has been my contention that determination and drive always yield desire. And without desire, daily routine tasks can become cumbersome. It is the mundane and everyday undertakings that stress us out and put a damper on our spirit.

As you will read in a later chapter, one of the most earth-shattering experiences I have ever had occurred when I was an underwriter, which is one of the most important jobs in banking. However, for me, it was meaningless. It was an anchor of stress wrapped around my neck because I did not enjoy it, and quite frankly, I was not good at it. Underwriting was not my passion because it was not my purpose.

I am a speaker, author, life coach, and workshop facilitator. I love what I do. I know what I want out of life, and I know that my talents and the people I surround myself with will lead me on this journey we call life. My purpose is fueled by my desires.

What about you?

1. What is the one thing you really want out of life?
2. How badly do you want it?
3. What are you willing to do to get it?

REFLECTIONS

CHAPTER 2

DEFINING VISION

Having a personal vision is the next and most essential step to defining your destiny. It is the dreams of men and women that have sparked the rise of human existence. The Reverend Dr. Martin Luther King, Jr. had a dream. John F. Kennedy—putting a man on the moon. Abraham Lincoln—a free society for all men and women. Bill Gates—a computer in every home. Nelson Mandela—equality in South Africa; and Mahatma Gandhi had a similar vision for India. These were ordinary people who had big dreams and inspired generations to change the course of history for millions of people. The world, as we know it, is the culmination of great vision with the ability to dream.

If you are a leader, and I believe we all are, you must paint a vision large enough to motivate, not just yourself, but the people in your sphere of influence. Martin Luther King, Jr. did not stand on the steps of the Lincoln Memorial on a sweltering summer day in 1963 and proclaim to the world, "I have a strategic plan." No, he said, "I have a dream." People will follow someone with a dream, and the bigger the better. As Bill Turner, founding member of the Pastoral Institute likes to say, "No one gets inspired by a small vision."

As my work has grown over the years, I have had the privilege of meeting some outstanding leaders. I have gotten to know extroverts as well as introverts; assertive leaders, who are seen as "driving and telling," and those who are peacekeepers by nature; females and males; doctors, attorneys, ministers, school superintendents, musical directors, coaches, and teachers. On the other hand, I have come across leaders who are not in positions of formal leadership. They are fathers, mothers, aunts, uncles, grandfathers, and grandmothers. Regardless of their influence, because that is what leadership is, they all had a strong desire to do great things, and they each had an impeccable vision.

A strong vision can change the world because it galvanizes the masses. Establishing your personal vision should be one of the first things you do when embarking on a major endeavor. Most Americans live in the Red Zone—working an average of 46 hours a week (not including the extra time in the morning when they have to rise early to get the kids to school, be at work on time themselves, run errands during lunch, and everything after work such as preparing dinner, PTA, soccer, dance classes, and helping with homework). With all of these activities going on in a given week, and in some cases, a single day, it is understandable how the big picture of your own personal desires can easily get lost.[2]

Your vision need not be as big as Dr. King's, but it is your North Star. It paints the picture and keeps you focused so you do not lose sight of where you are going.

---

[2] John Ryan, The Three Fundamentals of Leadership, *Forbes*, April 29, 2009, http://www.forbes.com/2009/04/29/vision-communication-judgment-leadership-managing-ccl.html

Once you begin dreaming, your imagination will take over. On the other hand, if you don't do it, you might not fail, but it is doubtful you will reach the heights of your capabilities. Meditate on the service you want to provide, the person you want to become, and the things you want to do. Whatever it may be, it is up to you and no one else. The purpose is to propel you to the next level, and only you will know what that truly looks like.

Attaching significance to your dream is paramount if you want it to come to fruition, because achievement means different things to different people. That is why you will have to answer the all-important "why" question. "Why" are you contemplating these grand thoughts of yours? What works for you may not work for me.

No matter how big your thinking, it can always get bigger. If you want to raise the bar, if you want to serve the world, or if you want to change the world, you must first dream it before you can see it.[3]

When I left Synovus, I needed a little extra motivation, something to keep me focused, so I created my first vision board. I purchased a poster and subsequently placed the images of six things on it that I desired to accomplish. The last visuals I saw before going to bed each night, and the first graphics I saw when I woke up, were those pictures. In due time, I achieved five of them. To this day, I still find it interesting the one endeavor I didn't attain: I had a depiction of me hosting a radio show. Instead, I eventually had my own television show.

The World Wide Web has made my single-mindedness of purpose easier. I have a digital board of sorts on my Pinterest account, so

---

[3] Daniel Burrus, "Think Big… and Then Think Bigger," *Huffington Post*, Apr. 3, 2013, http://www.huffingtonpost.com/daniel-burrus/think-bigand-then-think-b_b_3007689.html

when I need a little boost to escape for a few minutes during the day, I pull up the site and look at my pins.

I wanted to take it to an even higher level, so I called a consultant friend of mine to help me put together my own personal vision statement—everything—the way I think, feel, my whole being. I was asked several questions about what I wanted out of life, and each time I provided him with an answer, he would ask me the all-important "Why" question. Why do you want that? Why is that important to you? Why? Why? Why? It was exhausting, but he wanted me to be as specific as possible. It worked, because I now have a clearer picture of who I am, what I want, and why I want it. It must be noted I am well aware that as my life changes, so might my vision.

For now, here is my personal vision statement:

> I am an agent of positive change in the world.
> I do so in the following arenas:
> I love, nurture and provide for my daughters.
> I devote my professional time and energy to introducing individuals and institutions to the value of self-awareness and provide them with the tools for their own journeys.

I continuously hone my own self-awareness practice so I might better serve as a role model and teacher.

Word of Caution

There are consequences to thinking big, and you must be prepared. Having a huge dream and a "keen pulsating" desire can easily scare away the very people you love the most. So, it is vital that you are careful about the people you surround yourself with, which is something I will discuss in detail in a later chapter. Not everyone in your sphere of influence has the wherewithal to imagine the possibilities and impossibilities of life. It is also unfathomable for some people to dream big or even buy into your vision, let alone one of their own, and they may be indifferent to whether you succeed or fail. I have observed that, for whatever reason, there are individuals who are afraid to dream. They are caught up living their day-to-day existence—they wake up each morning, go to work at a job with no meaning or purpose, and do the same things every day—and they are always one step closer to the dreams and goals they do not have. Be watchful of these people: whether knowingly or unknowingly, they can sabotage your dreams.

Remember to embrace your vision. Coincidently, do you know who has the best dreams? Children. Yes, children. They have the purest of imaginations. You can go into any neighborhood in America, the suburbs, out in the country, Main Street U.S.A. or the projects, and ask children what they want to be when they grow up, and they will sincerely look you in the eye and tell you.

Show me a man or woman who has done great things, and I will show you a person who dreamed big. They could envision themselves doing the things in life they endeavored to accomplish. Not only did they imagine their success, but they worked hard each and every day to achieve their desires. Perhaps this is why my heart always goes out to the person who can no longer dream.

Every achiever I have ever met was like an artist. When I talked to them about their purpose in life, the picture they painted of their being was crystal clear. If you want to live a life of meaning, you must have a strong vision of who you are and what you want. If I did not have the ability to dream big (and we all do), I probably would have quit my journey a long time ago, but I still have much work to do.

I had many dreams when I was growing up. As far back as I can remember, I wanted to play high school basketball for my dad, college basketball for an NCAA championship program, and for the Los Angeles Lakers in the National Basketball Association. Due to a few genetic challenges—slightly shorter than six feet tall, occasionally overweight, and a tad bit slow—those dreams never materialized.

Another dream of mine was to see more of this great country of ours. Oddly enough, it began with my wanting to visit Chicago, Illinois. When I was growing up in my small town in east Alabama, I had many relatives who moved to the Midwest during the time of the great migration to find prosperity and get away from the cotton mills and farm life. From an early age, practically everyone I knew spoke glowingly about living "up North," so it was ingrained in me from the outset to want to visit the big city just as they did.

Chicago is one of my favorite cities in the world. Having had the opportunity to speak there makes it even more special.

My immediate family did not travel much when I was a child. Most of the places I visited, until the age of 18, were confined to the state of Alabama and perhaps West Central Georgia. As the son of a coach, whenever the team traveled, I usually went with them, as did my mom and sister.

My biggest thrill as it related to travel was awaiting visits from relatives who came from the Midwest, and it did not matter which side of the family they were on. The anticipation and excitement was the same. I remember summer nights being awakened in the wee hours of the morning so we could all jump in the car for a ride to the Columbus Metropolitan Airport to pick up a family member. Or, when my relatives drove "down South" in their big shiny cars and my sister and I waited with bated breath for their arrival.

My Grandmother Izora had pictures of the Windy City on the walls of her living room. They were the original version of my vision board. I would lie on the sofa, with the television blaring, and stare at those photographs. I wondered what it was like to live there. Years later, I thought about those pictures when I started working at Total System Services. During the first five years of my employment with the data processing company, I visited Chi-Town on numerous occasions. Each time I went I couldn't help but think of the photos in my grandmother's home. One of my earliest dreams had become a reality.

A Friend with No Vision

In the King James Version of the Bible, Proverbs 28:19 says, "Where there is no vision, the people perish."

When I was a freshman in college, I got a part-time summer job at a fast-food restaurant. While there, I met a fellow student named Doug. We hit it off immediately. He was from a small community not far from my hometown. He came from a big family and had lots of brothers and sisters. Although I did not know him while I was in high school, we did have a couple of mutual friends.

Oftentimes, Doug and I studied together. He was a good student. The two of us spent a lot of time together talking about life. While I lived in an off-campus apartment at Auburn, Doug commuted the 45-minute drive and spent his idle time at our apartment studying and shootin' the breeze.

During the latter part of the winter quarter of our junior year, I was sitting in my apartment along with my roommate and a couple of other guys. We were having a serious discussion about politics, world events, and visions of our future. It was a lively discourse. Everyone was talking with the exception of Doug.

"Why are you so quiet, Doug?" I asked.

"I don't know. I just am," he said.

We continued to talk, and 15 minutes later it happened. "I think I am going to drop out of school," he mumbled, with a hint of exasperation. He was barely audible, but I heard him and so did everyone else. "You're gonna WHAT?" my roommate screamed at the top of his lungs in disbelief.

"I am going to drop out of school," Doug said, this time more matter-of-fact but still somewhat timidly.

"Why do you want to that?" my roommate asked with annoyance.

"I'm going to buy a car," said Doug.

"But Doug, you are just a year and a half from graduating," I said, almost pleading.

We continued to talk to Doug, but he had already made up his mind. The next week he called it quits.

I graduated college less than two years later and began working at Total System Services almost right away. One of the first things I did was buy a car. Five years later I was driving through the old neighborhood and saw Doug at a high school classmate's house. I stopped and chatted with them for a few minutes. I noticed Doug was driving the same vehicle he had talked about purchasing that day he came to the apartment. He was also wearing the same fast-food restaurant uniform.

Doug's decision to quit school baffled me. Yes, there are cases that call for doing such a thing, but he was not in that type of predicament. Whatever you do, do not stop dreaming. It is your North Star. Take the time to look toward the heavens and envision yourself doing the things in life in which you want. Your ability to dream and have a truer vision of yourself will propel you forward. Use your imagination because in your dreams, you always triumph.

What about you?

1. How big is your vision?
2. Where do you see yourself a year from now?
3. Where do you see yourself five years from now?
4. Do you remember what you wanted to be when you were a child?
5. Did you achieve your dreams? If so, that is great. If not, why not? What happened?

Reflections

CHAPTER 3

DEFINING EDUCATION

Ninety percent of Americans think college is essential for career opportunities, while 67 percent consider education the key to competitiveness in the global economy. This is according to research conducted by the Career College Association. During tough economic times, education may be the main ingredient in keeping your job or finding a new one. The unemployment rate in October 2009 for people with a bachelor's degree or higher was 4.6 percent but for people without a degree the unemployment rate was 14 percent. Anything over 10 percent is considered to be high. Forty-two percent of all learners in 2001 were over the age of 25. The fastest growing group of the higher education population is adult learners.[4]

---

[4] Pamela Rutledge, "Want to Keep Your Job? Get More Education," *Psychology Today*, (2009), http://www.psychologytoday.com/blog/positively-media/200911/want-keep-your-job-get-more-education

As technology and society advance in the years to come, more significance will be placed on earning a college degree. At this writing, nearly 100 million American jobs demand advanced skills. However, less than 50 million Americans have the necessary qualifications to fill these positions. By the end of the decade, more than 60 percent of all U.S. jobs will call for some usage of postsecondary education.[5]

We spend a great deal of our time the first twenty-two years of our life in classrooms "just" learning. I have met young people who think that as soon as they get their diploma or degree, their time in school is over and they are ready for the real world, but that is simply not how life works. This is a rather weird mindset. Just think about it. You come into this world and you are expected to attend school until you are 18 or 22 years of age, and after that you are not expected to attend another class for the rest of your life, which if you are fortunate, will be at least 40-50 more years. So, does that mean for the next four or five decades you are going to fall behind the rest of society, if younger people keep graduating from the education system and bringing new ideas into the world?

Your formal education is not the only form of learning. Many men and women are autodidacts—those who dedicate themselves to self-education, either in addition to or as a replacement for their formal education. My mother, grandmother, and numerous relatives fit into this category. All of them read the Bible, the newspaper, and other periodicals that constantly improved their knowledge level.

Education has always been important in my family. Both of my parents were valedictorians of their respective high school classes.

---

[5] Julia Smith, "The Growing Importance of Education in the Job Market," *Value of Education* (blog), March 21, 2013, http://blog.online.colostate.edu/blog/value-of-education/growing-importance-of-education-in-the-job-market/

My father received his master's degree from Fisk University in Nashville, Tennessee. If he had not fallen in love with coaching basketball, I am sure he would have pursued a PhD.

My mother never went to college but she raised two children who did. My sister, Krystal, and I, both graduated from Auburn University. We both have master's degrees, and she is currently pursuing a doctorate. This is not meant to try to impress you but to impress upon you just how important learning is to my family.

I had been in the workforce and out of college for nearly 12 years before I decided to return to school and get my master's degree. It turned out to be one of the most rewarding experiences of my life. To have my daughters watch me walk across the stage and receive that piece of paper was priceless.

If I could pinpoint one thing that gave me an edge in my life, however, it would be my insatiable appetite for reading. I never made straight A's while in school, but reading was and still is something I really enjoy.

My late paternal grandmother, Izora Redd, was an avid reader. Her favorite saying when it came to anything that was happening in the news was, "The paper said..." If it was in the *Columbus Ledger-Enquirer*, she read it, and it was the gospel. When I was a senior in high school, I told her I was applying for a job at a local retail store. Before I could finish my sentence, she filled in the blanks by telling me where the store was located and what job was open. How did she know? She had already read the want ads in the morning paper.

My grandmother, Izora Redd, loved to read the daily newspaper. If something was going on in the community, she certainly knew about it.

My father also loved to read. Books and magazines filled our home. Dad subscribed to periodicals like *Omni, Psychology Today, Time* and *Newsweek,* and the Sunday edition of the *New York Times.* After a while, we'd have so many magazines piled up around the house that he would put them in shopping bags and take them to his brothers, so they could read them.

Always take advantage of furthering your education—formal or otherwise. Several years ago, my former manager, Fran, suggested I get certified in Emergenetics. I told her I didn't want to, and she didn't press the issue. Several months later she came into my office and suggested it again. And again, I said no. However, this time, in her logical and well-thought-out manner, she said, "Kelvin, this is an opportunity for you to add another tool to your toolbox. Whenever you get such an opportunity, especially if your company is going to pay for it, you should take it." That was all it took. It made so much sense. No one can deny that we are living in uncertain economic times. Whenever the opportunity presents itself for you to gain more knowledge, add more tools to your toolbox, take advantage of it. You never know when you may need them.[6]

I aspire to be a lifelong learner. In so many ways, the essence of *Define Your Destiny* is all about the many lessons, formal and informal, that I have learned in my lifetime. No matter what I do, good or bad, there is a message to be gained from it.

Think

In the 1980s, my dad's basketball team had a huge game against one of our conference rivals. The winner would advance to the state tournament.

"It's an honor to be picked to coach the all-stars, but winning the state championship is more important to me." James B. Redd

Redd To Coach South 3A-4A Stars

I am very blessed to have grown up with a strong father figure in my life.

After three quarters of play, the game was tied. The lead went back and forth. But early in the fourth quarter with five minutes left in

---

[6] Brett McKay and Kate McKay, "How and Why to Become a Lifelong Learner," *Art of Manliness* (blog), March 18, 2013, http://www.artofmanliness.com/2013/03/18/how-and-why-to-become-a-lifelong-learner/

the game, we were not playing very well and found ourselves losing by double digits. The crowd was growing restless and weary. I was sitting in the bleachers behind my dad, and I looked at him and he was uncharacteristically just sitting there with his chin in his hands. I had never seen him do that —just sit there. He then began to substitute the first team players for the second team. I literally thought he was blowing the game, and I had never felt that way before.

The second team actually played well. When we finally caught up to our opponents, my father substituted the starters back into the game. We eventually took the lead and won an extremely close contest.

Afterward, when we were at home, I asked Dad why was he so motionless while we were losing and there was not much time left to play.

He said, "I was thinking."

Still, to this day, his answer amazes me. There was so much chaos and the gym was so loud from the crowd noise. Our players were making one mistake after another, and he was "thinking." He said he needed to gather his thoughts. In retrospect, I am not surprised by his actions. He is a person who has a preference for analytical thinking, and he does process things internally, but what a lesson in leadership. In that instance, it worked. I learned a lot about the importance of "thinking" from that game and our subsequent conversation.

When things are not going well for me, I cannot begin to tell you how often I take a step back to gather my thoughts. I do this in myriad ways. Sometimes I take long drives in my car. Other times I walk in my neighborhood or at one of my favorite nature spots.

There are times I feel like "thinking" is a lost art. Spiritually, the Bible says, "Peace! Be still." I do not want to use this in the wrong context, but I wonder how many people actually take the time to just "be"?

What about you?

1. What tools are you presently putting in your toolbox?
2. What is your favorite means of educating yourself?
3. Do you ever set aside time to just "be"?

REFLECTIONS

CHAPTER 4

DEFINING SELF-AWARENESS

When organizations ask me to conduct a servant leadership training and development program, I try to begin with a self-assessment—usually Emergenetics, a brain-based approach to personality profiling. I want the participants to gain insight into their strengths and weaknesses. To lead effectively, you must have a powerful sense of self—an understanding of who you are. Failure to take the time to analyze yourself will ultimately derail your personal development process.

When I began my career at the Pastoral Institute, I was introduced to five of the most important questions necessary for a person who wants to embark on the journey toward self-awareness.

Who am I? This is an age-old question that man asks when he is in search of himself. What is my reason for "being"? Once you begin to ponder this question, the answer may not come immediately. It may take years of reflection. I did not begin to even contemplate it until I was in my mid- to late 30s. Of course, there are those who discover the answer to this question at an earlier age.

If someone had told me twenty years ago that I would one day work at the Pastoral Institute, I wouldn't have believed it. But this has been one of the most rewarding work experiences I have ever had.

Why am I here? As you continue to meditate on the first question, the answer to this one will become clearer. I met a man once who looked good "on paper." He had a beautiful wife and two kids and lived in a nice neighborhood. He also had a good salary, but he complained incessantly about his 60- to 70-hour workweeks. After telling me his story, the first question he asked me was: Is this all there is? He no longer wanted to work extra-long hours in a job he didn't love. After much reflection, he left his company to pursue his passion.

What makes me unique? You are born with at least one talent that makes you "uniquely you." It is up to you to find out what it is, but you must be honest with yourself. I know this from experience. There is nothing like being a speaker in the world of underwriters. What is the one thing you do well? When have you received a compliment for doing it? Discovering, maintaining, and honing your gift is the secret to defining your destiny. Focus your time and energy on what you do best. Great joy comes from using innate talents.

Where am I going? It is a big world out there. Where in it can you use your talent(s)? I am a firm believer that when you find the answers to the other four questions, the Universe will find a place for you, so do not be concerned about what others are doing or where others are going. Everyone's path to triumph and self-actualization is different. Don't spend time sweating the small stuff, worrying when others' journeys take them on a dissimilar path.

Who am I going to take with me? To paraphrase Jim Collins, bestselling author of the book *Good to Great*, you have to make sure the right people are on your bus and in the right seats. And not everyone belongs on your bus. You have been given the keys to your future. You are the driver. You must be extremely guarded about who is allowed to come along for the ride. The sign on your bus should read: "First-Class Seats for First Class People Only." This should be your attitude when it comes to inviting people into your life. They are not necessarily meant to ride the bus for the duration of the trip, and it is up to you to make sure they are seated properly.

Don't Take Your Talents for Granted

When I was in my late 20s, I became disillusioned with speaking about topics on motivation and leadership. I wondered if I was getting my message across to my audience. I did not think I was, so I stopped speaking altogether.

About a year later, my boss asked me to conduct a series of presentations with him. Our division was rather large. He wanted to speak to every employee but if he had to do it by himself, he thought it would be too tiring. With the two of us presenting together, we could conduct several presentations over the course of four hours and reach everyone. Of course, I said yes, and I thanked him for the opportunity. It was no big deal to me, and I did not think anything of it. I was used to speaking in front of groups, but this would be the first time I would be speaking in quite a while. I was surprised by what was in store for me.

On the morning of the presentation, I walked into the big conference room with my boss. We sat down. We talked and waited for the first wave of employees to arrive. He was used to speaking in public, and he was quite good at it. He had, as they say, "the gift of gab." A half-hour later the first round of employees strolled in and took their seats. My boss spoke first and did an outstanding job. Then it was my turn. I stood up and walked toward the front of the room. To this day, I will never forget what happened to me next. I started shaking all over, and my voice quivered. My heart was beating so hard and fast I could literally hear it.

After the first group left the conference room, I sat down.

Get a grip. You are Kelvin Redd, and you are used to speaking in front of people. Come on, man. Get a grip, I said to myself, as I tried to gather my nerves, but it did not work.

That feeling stayed with me the entire morning. I had not spoken in nearly 12 months, and it showed.

Mothers have a way of seeing things in their children that their children cannot see for themselves. Months before that morning with my boss, my mom had been trying to refocus my attention on speaking. If it had not been for her, I probably never would have returned to the podium, but she would not allow me to stop. She would constantly say to me, "Kelvin, son, you have a gift. You need to use it. If you don't use it, you will lose it." It was not until

I stood in front of my co-workers that morning in the big conference room that I realized what she had been trying to get through to me.

My encourager. My rock. My mother, Marie Redd. When all else fails, Mom will make it right.

From that day forward, I have never once presented without the goal of making a difference in someone's life by using the one gift I know God gave me. I am very intentional about my craft. I do not take it lightly.

Dealing with the Brutal Facts of Reality

If you want to define your destiny, you must be willing to confront and be watchful for the brutal facts of your own reality. Understanding who you are, what you can and cannot do, is based solely on how honest you are with yourself. No person ever achieved greatness without first developing a sound approach that was consistent with a truthful assessment of who he was.

In college, I majored in history and minored in business and communication. I had every intention of becoming a secondary education history teacher. I enjoyed studying the American past–African-American and European. More than likely, I would have pursued a master's degree and quite possibly a doctorate in education or history. During my senior year in college, one of my history professors even talked to me about applying for a fellowship to continue my studies. With three months remaining before graduation, I had two job offers in teaching and one in a museum, and then fate took over.

On a cold January morning in the winter of 1990, my mom was grocery shopping and ran into one of my dad's former students. "How's Kelvin doing?" he asked.

"He's doing fine. He's set to graduate in a couple of months," Mom said.

"Really? Listen, tell him that Total System Services is looking for some management associates, and if he's interested, to give me a call," he said.

My mother relayed the message to me. On a whim, I decided to apply for the job. A little less than five months later, on May 14, 1990, I began my career as a management associate at one of the world's largest bankcard processing companies, Total System Services, Inc. (now TSYS), a subsidiary of Synovus Financial Corp., in Columbus, Georgia.

I worked for all three of Synovus' major companies during my 13-year tenure with the organization. I spent seven years at Total System, three years at Synovus, and three years at Columbus Bank & Trust Company. I really enjoyed my time at Total System. It had a family atmosphere. Many of my friends still work there today.

Synovus has a special place in my heart. It's where I learned the importance of good management and great leadership.

The beginning of the end of my career at Synovus all started when I was walking through the lobby of CB&T. I had my head down, and when I looked up, I saw then-President Sam Wellborn. We had actually passed one another after a nod and brief hello, and then it happened.

"Kelvin," Sam yelled, standing at least five feet away from me as he turned around.

"Yes, sir," I said.

"Can you sell?" he asked inquisitively.

"I think I can. With all due respect, I created a safety program in a banking and data processing environment and was promoted to assistant vice president. So, yes, I think I can," I said with as much humility as I could.

"Have you ever thought about coming to work at the bank?" he asked.

"I have thought about it, but that was the extent of it. Just a thought," I said.

And that was it. He waved, nodded, and headed down the hall through the lobby.

After much discussion, a lot of self-doubt on my part, and three months later, I began my banking career at CB&T.

I enjoyed my time at Total System and Synovus. During my combined seven years with the two companies, I had only two managers, and they were near the top of the organizational chart, so I was afforded the privilege of having access to the company's brain trust, where I was introduced to servant leadership. My education in this setting was immense, but my career goals changed when I went to work at the bank.

I felt like my career began all over again when I joined CB&T. My training originated at the Bradley Park Branch. At the time, it was the bank's busiest location. The first thing I had to learn was how to become a teller. The teller training lasted a couple days before I was thrown to the wolves on the first Friday of the month. The branch was humming, as they say. I was doing okay until a local restaurateur challenged my math. I remember it like it was yesterday. He was standing at the back of the line when I heard him. "YOU SHORTED ME FIVE DOLLARS!" he yelled from the rear of the line in an angry tone.

At first, I did not know who he was talking to. Then he said it again.

"YOU SHORTED ME FIVE DOLLARS!" he yelled once more. This time he seemed angrier than before. He was certainly louder.

After the second yell, he broke the line and walked toward me. The head teller intercepted him about halfway. She took him aside. He explained to her what had happened. Evidently, when he was in the bank the day before, I had forgotten to give him his five dollars in dimes. He had come back to get his money. That was how my first week in banking went. That should have been a sign of things to come.

Customer service and training followed suit. This was a little bit better for me. I was able to use my communication skills and help a lot of customers. I enjoyed branch management training, too. I learned how to make consumer loans, much of which was based on the use of a checklist. Even then I had a preference for structural thinking, so that worked well for me. I also gained knowledge in managing the branch when the manager was not in the office. After nearly a year, it was time for me to move into the world of underwriting and the end of my career at Synovus was on the horizon.

My office was in the basement with no windows, and I found myself looking at financial sheets all day long. Underwriting is vital to any financial institution. It is an abstract and mostly left-brain thinking job, which did not play into my strengths at all. There were a lot of moving parts and no formulas or checklists to use like I had in consumer lending. I hated it because I simply could not connect the dots.

Going into the position, I really did not know what to expect, but I believed I would be able to handle it. I did know that underwriting was the training ground for becoming a commercial lender, which was one of the most coveted and elite positions in the bank. However, after about five months, I had to face the brutal facts of reality—I was not cut out for it.

When you do not enjoy your work, it negatively affects just about everything about you. I didn't enjoy going to work every day, and I take full responsibility for it, as it was a tremendous, albeit emotionally painful, learning experience that helped shaped my self-awareness philosophy. This is precisely why you will never hear me say to a child that "you can be or do anything in this world that you want to do." That is simply not true. If he does not have the talent to execute, he will not succeed. It is only setting the individual up to fail. I received confirmation of this fact at the 2010

Jim Blanchard Leadership Forum. Bestselling author Malcolm Gladwell was one of the guest speakers. He had just finished talking about his book *Outliers*. I was fortunate to be able to ask him a question during the Q&A period.

"Can a person be anything he wants to be in life?" I asked.

"Of course not. That is a ridiculous assertion. If he does not have the talent, he will not succeed. No matter how much I would like it, there is a reason I am not an NBA basketball player," he responded.

I cannot tell you how many times a student with no aptitude for science or math has told me he was going to major in engineering. Or the parent who thinks that his child should be the starting quarterback on the football team as a sophomore when the kid who is actually starting, a senior, is being recruited by every major college in his region.

In order to be effective in anything, you must have a deep understanding of your strengths AND your limitations. If you fail to do that, you will fail. Coming to grips with the brutal facts of reality is a necessary part of the self-awareness journey.

Vulnerability

University of Houston professor Dr. Brene Brown says, "We cultivate love when we allow our most vulnerable and powerful selves to be deeply seen and known, and when we honor the spiritual connection that grows from that offering with trust, respect, kindness and affection."

The idea of expressing my vulnerability was suggested to me by a friend. I was apprehensive at first, until I learned that the alter ego of vulnerability is courage. That is the point about servant leadership that I absolutely love. It forces you to take a hard look at yourself, which is a necessary part of your growth.

I am discovering my own vulnerabilities because I want to reach my higher self and be a better person. When people meet me for the first time, I would like for them to say, "He's real."

It has been liberating. I am who I am, and I am growing comfortable with it. My vulnerabilities clarify my values. I know what I like. I know what I do not like. I know what I stand for, and I know what I stand against.

From time to time, I am asked, "What does vulnerability have to do with servant leadership?" My answer: Everything. In truth, it takes an enormous amount of nerve and audacity to express our vulnerabilities. To put ourselves "out there" is daunting. All servant leaders foster this unique part of their being. Not only do they know who they are, but they honor it. Vulnerability is the highest form of authenticity, which makes it the highest form of self-awareness. The servant leader understands who he was and who he is and that he is in a continual state of becoming. It is a part of the venture that never ends.

The discovery of one's self is the underlying purpose of *Discover Your Destiny*, warts and all, as I stated in my first book, *Stand Tall: Essays on Life and Servant Leadership*. The true essence of servant leadership will unsettle you just as it did me when I began my journey over two decades ago. One day I looked in the mirror, and I questioned who I was. To be 'deeply seen and known'? Are you kidding me? That was not a good feeling and occasionally when I get out of balance, it is still some scary stuff but again, I am reminded to take a good a hard look at myself.

People tend to only know the surface-level aspects of the term servant leadership—trust, persuasion, conceptualization, humility, listening, etc. Those are the basics, but each quality of a servant leader, when studied in-depth, is more educational and spiritual in nature and has a deeper meaning.

I have observed that most people have a "you must think like me" attitude and if you do not "think like me," then something is wrong with you. Obviously, if you are on the journey toward servant leadership, this is not your mindset because you honor differences in thought. You understand that what may be good for the goose may not be good for the gander and that our distinctions are what make us unique and set us apart from everything and everyone else.

Society is homogeneous in nature. The people we tend to associate with are just like us, and we see them every day whether in our neighborhood, at church, school, or work, so there is a tendency for the individuality of the person to get lost. Our differences get metamorphosed into the group and we forget who we are.

Cast Down Your Bucket Where You Are

When I was a management associate at Total System, I was teamed with six other trainees. Our task was to visit and spend time in every division. We were together almost every day.

Then, one Friday afternoon, I was called in to see the Vice President of Human Resources. She said the company needed to get control of its insurance premiums and one of the best ways to do that was to establish a safety program, and she wanted me to work on it as a project.

I was crushed. Safety? *I did not go to college to work in safety*, I said to myself. I went home that weekend and thought of resigning. A friend of mine, who had a manufacturing background, believed it was a wonderful move. I thought otherwise.

Once again, I had to do some serious soul searching. I began by asking myself a question: How can I turn this work into something promising? I went to the library and did a lot of reading. The first thing I noticed was that safety involved a lot of training and education, and that actually appealed to me.

When I arrived at work the following Monday morning, I threw my whole being into the job. I had decided I was going to utilize my strengths. I focused all of my efforts on the training and education aspects of the position and set out to establish the first-ever company-wide safety program.

I set up a safety committee that consisted of having at least one monitor and an alternate in every department throughout the organization. I had the blessing of the CEO and was fortunate to meet with him at least 2-3 times a year. No other MA had that type of access.

I established a monthly newsletter called *Safety First*. Several of the divisions within the company had their own magazines, like *DataLink*. I wrote articles for that and other publications. On numerous occasions, customers read the articles and inquired about our safety program. As a result, I began traveling the country, speaking to our clients.

I presented an average of fifty presentations a year, including one every six months to executive management. As the program grew, I was asked to speak at the bank, the holding company, and the affiliates.

Being a safety director in a banking and data processing environment was not the easiest thing in the world. I heard my share of jokes. That is why I always endeavored to do things first class and be the best I could be whenever I presented to my co-workers. Oftentimes, I succeeded and it showed when in 1995, I was promoted to assistant vice president and Director of Safety. I was now responsible for a safety program in five states and Mexico.

Of course, it did not hurt my cause that I had Lynn Drury, my manager, in my corner. He had been a former assistant to the president of a major Fortune 500 company. He was a true professional and guided me every step of the way my first 14 months in safety. I wrote about him extensively in *Stand Tall: Essays on Life and Servant Leadership*. The chapter is titled, "The Mentor."

In 1895, Booker T. Washington coined the phrase, "Cast Down Your Bucket Where You Are." It means, "You need to make do with what you have and make the best of it and everything will be OK." That is exactly how I approached my responsibilities when I was told to establish a safety program for Total System. Once I got over the shame of being the "safety guy" in a high-tech environment, I realized that the position, regardless of the title, lined up perfectly with my skill sets, and it was "full steam ahead" from that point on. However, this whole experience was a huge lesson in humility for me.

The safety director's job was a great training ground for me. I learned how to write, develop a newsletter, prepare a marketing plan, and present to, establish, and maintain working relationships with different types of groups—first line employees, middle managers, executive management, non-company employees, and various community groups. I learned that if I was charged with a safety program in a banking and data processing company and the employees did not know about it, neither the safety program nor I would survive, so I made sure everyone knew that we had one. Basically, everything I am doing now, I did then. All you have to do is remove the name "safety," and insert "servant leadership," and it's the same process. As the safety director and now the Director of the Center for Servant Leadership, I have traveled all across this great country of ours as well as internationally using my talents.

Although I did not know it at the time, it took tremendous vulnerability for me to take the safety position in that type of work environment. I learned, even then, that expressing my true self, vulnerabilities and all, is at the heart and the development of understanding who I am.

Fortunately, I learned early on in the process the courage and the importance of using my talents, which was pretty raw at the time.

You have been given a gift. It is called a talent. It is uniquely you, and it can take you many places. Your talent is a gift to you from God. What you do with that talent is your gift back to Him.

What about you?

1. Have you discovered your talents? If so, are you using your talents?
2. Are you honest with yourself regarding your talents?
3. What does it mean for you to be vulnerable?
4. Do you have the courage to be vulnerable?

REFLECTIONS

CHAPTER 5

DEFINING RELATIONSHIPS: CHOOSE YOUR FRIENDS WITH CARE

There is nothing like having a good friend—someone to depend on, to talk to in good times as well as in bad. In some cases, a pal is better than a family member because he or she may know things about you that no one else does. All friendships, however, are not good, and many of our downfalls are due to the relationships in our lives.

How rare is a true friend? It depends on who you ask. Some would say true friends are extremely uncommon. One may think that a close friend might know everything there is to know about you but according to a study conducted by Weylin Sternglanz and Bella DePaulo, your very close friends are actually less likely to know your deep and emotional feelings. That is because your close friends are too emotionally tied to the friendship and might not ever notice the reality of the person you are or the situation you are involved in. Your close friends hold the 'ideal' or romanticized image of you. This might not be a bad thing, as many psychologists often tell couples to create a positive image of their significant other instead of a negative one.

Any relationship that has the influence to make us feel good can also make us feel bad. From the uncertain to the awful, friends come in all types. According to author and British sociologist Carlin Flora, "Friendfluence is the powerful and often unappreciated role that friends—past and present—play in determining our sense of self and the direction of our lives." It is so dominant that our friends can just as effortlessly have depressing effects as constructive ones. Even thoughtful, like-minded acquaintances can aggravate or harm us. And the fluid, innate traits of friendship are sometimes harder to deal with than the loving, passionate kind or even the people in our families.

Friends may have the best of intentions but they may also come with harmful power over you. These are friends whose dreams, ideals, or way of life are not in alignment with yours and it is when the relationship is at its peak that you could lose sight of who you are because of your close association with them. If you become aware of what is happening, you will begin to make preparations to avoid these toxic relationships.

However, people who lack self-awareness do not understand what is best for them, so they will lean toward doing things that others do. You see them get involved in relationships that are not good for them—getting married because it is what their friends are doing, choosing a career path that does not bode well for their talents. Many of these decisions are enhanced simply by the type of people they are surrounded by.

Individuals who have your best interests at heart—those who affirm and authenticate who you are—boost your self-esteem with ease. On the other hand, if you surround yourself with people who are only interested in their own emotional well-being (the "energy drainers"), you will find yourself climbing uphill in the relationship.

Flora conducted a poll of a thousand people and discovered that almost two-thirds identified friends as one of the biggest sources of stress in their lives. There is the friend who constantly wears you out in every conversation by telling you all of his problems or the co-dependent friend who calls you at every waking hour of the day and night. Although they can be great, at times they are annoying. Friends are also the chief source of discontent with companions and relatives. The late British sociologist Ray Pahl's research points out that "Friends are the main cause of arguments with partners and families." And then there are those people you befriend but they do not add value to your life. They are not positive or negative. They are just there.[7]

I can tell a lot about a person by the company he keeps. Several years ago, I befriended Morgan. We had lots of dinners together and long talks about politics, sports, religion, and just about everything else under the sun. Our conversations were legendary, but there was something about our rapport that disturbed me. When he was not around me, he hung out with a couple of guys who were rumored to be troublemakers. Pretty soon his relationship with them was telling, as they found themselves in some serious trouble and because of his association with them, so did Morgan.

I learned a huge lesson from my time spent with Morgan that still serves me today. My friendship with "you" is not solely predicated

---

[7] Carlin Flora, "The Mix Bag Buddy and Other Friendship Conundrums," *Psychology Today, (2013),* http://www.psychologytoday.com/articles/201212/ the-mixed-bag-buddy-and-other-friendship-conundrums

on how you treat me, but equally important it is who you spend time with when you are not in my presence.

Please do not get me wrong. I am not some holier-than-thou individual. On the contrary, I am simply very selective as to whom I allow into my inner sanctum. I am guided by my favorite Bible scripture, Proverbs 13:20, which says, "He who walks with wise men shall be wise but a companion of fools shall be destroyed." In every speech I give that pertains to relationships, I repeat this verse. If I am in a non-religious setting I simply say, "Birds of a feather flock together." Typically, I quote it to young people but I am amazed at how pertinent it is for adults, too.

Have I made mistakes by surrounding myself with people who are bad influences? Yes, indeed, but I would like to think I have a good batting average on the positive side of friendships. For a while, especially when I was in my teens, I suffered from the "I-want-to-be-liked" syndrome. Fortunately for me, I grew out of it. I have a yellow streak down the middle of my back that is a mile long in terms of the people I surround myself with. For those of you who do not know, that means that I am afraid of being around unsavory people. You can say a lot of things about Kelvin Redd (I know, third person), but you can never say that you have seen me hanging out with the wrong crowd. That ain't gonna happen. I value myself too much to allow destructive people in my life.

Be Nice

Being nice or kind is doing something without expecting a return. Kindness and love are two sides of the same coin. Compassion is authority in its constructive appearance—just as meanness is authority in its unconstructive appearance. Doing something for someone else because you look forward to their returning the favor is not compassion or the act of being nice. It's a deal, a premeditated move or maybe even exploitation.[8]

Servant leadership is a way of life, and when I worked for Synovus Financial Corp., they were voted in 1999 as the Best Place to Work in America by *Fortune* magazine, due to the organization's strong belief in the world's most powerful leadership philosophy. The enterprise placed special emphasis on service to its customers—internal and external.

During my transition from Synovus Financial Corp. to Columbus Bank and Trust Company, I had the opportunity to meet with the CEO, Steve Melton. At the time, the move was a major transition in my life, so I was bit pensive.

I had known Steve for a couple of years. As always, he was a gracious host. We talked about everything under the sun—sports, life, education, family, and banking. Nearly an hour passed before our meeting concluded. He stood up from behind his desk and walked me to the door.

I will never forget his parting words when he said, "Kelvin, we can teach you to be a banker. We can't teach you to be a nice person." It was another one of those freeze-framed moments.

Research shows that 87 percent of our success is due to our people skills. That is why I am still so amazed by folks who do not get it. I have seen doctors who are awesome at their craft but have poor bedside manners. I know of teachers who can work their way through a quadratic formula but are despised by their pupils, parents, and co-workers. I know of managers who can recite the company's policy manual frontwards and backwards but cannot

---

[8] Rosemary Sword, "Kindness is the Key," *Psychology Today*, (2013), http://www.psychologytoday.com/blog/the-time-cure/201307/kindness-is-the-key

tell you anything but the name, rank, and serial number of their employees.

I would hope that everyone is nice. I realize that we all have our moments when we are not, but if you are in a formal position of leadership, your relational intelligence, just as much if not more than your technical skills, will determine the altitude of your success.

Don't Be a Snake Charmer

Most leaders I have come in contact with want to be liked. After all, they are human, but I have observed those who try too hard. They don't realize that some situations cry for something completely different. And in a moment's lapse in judgment, in their continual 'state of becoming,' they fall victim to their own insatiable need to empathize.

Years ago, there was an old man who had a vast amount of land. Every day he walked his property. On one cold January morning, he put on his winter clothes, scarf, and big coat, and proceeded to stroll his acreage. The farther he got away from his home, the colder it became, and snowflakes began to fall.

As he walked the hillside, he saw something moving ever so slightly in the brush. He bent down to have a closer look. It was a snake, and it was frozen stiff from the cold.

"Aww," the old man said as he picked up the reptile, looked at it, cradled it, placed it in his bosom and continued his morning trek.

After a while, the old man grew tired, so he began his walk back down the hillside. The closer he got to his house, the less cold it became. The snake began to thaw and the old man felt it move, so he opened his coat and gazed at the creature. "Aww...," the old man said with all the compassion in the world.

It was at the moment that the snake reared his head, looked the old man right in the eyes, showed his large fangs and bit the old man squarely in the chest. He fell to the ground writhing in immense pain.

With the snake sitting atop his chest and staring at him intently, the old man, stuttering and gasping for his last breath, said, "But, but...how could you?"

The snake, with an evil grin and showing his huge fangs, said, "You knew I was a snake when you picked me up."

The old man in the story was kind and caring but there are some people who just do not belong in our lives. These are the people I greet with a, "Hi, how are you? Bye, see you later." Realizing that not everyone is going to like you is essential to being true to yourself. Select people to be in your life who are worthy of being there. I am pretty sure you know who they are. I would rather spend time alone than be around someone who is going to emotionally shorten my lifespan.

Can You Trust Your Number Two?

No servant leadership or self-awareness book would be complete without a word on trust. No matter how big or small the institution, establishing and maintaining trust is the most important responsibility of a leader. All other endeavors like teambuilding, strategic planning, employee performance, and planning the office holiday party, fail without trust. Whether in business or in life, trust is the foundation of all relationships, and developing it is not as easy as it may appear. In order for trust to grow, both parties must know in their hearts that the other party has a genuine interest in them—that he or she is dedicated and truly cares. But devastating consequences can arise when the parties are in an environment that calls for them to closely work together and one party abuses the sacredness of trust. A lot has been written about an employee trusting his leader. However, what happens when the leader cannot trust the employee?

Matthew, one of the first ten original employees, became an established leader in the XYZ Corporation, which now boasted employment of nearly 2,000.

Matthew received numerous awards during his twelve-year tenure. He was highly respected inside and outside of the organization. He appeared in the local newspaper ten times in one calendar year and two national magazines ran stories on him.

It was during Matthew's sixth year with XYZ that Barnabas was hired. Barnabas made it no secret that he greatly admired Matthew's work. One day while in the cafeteria, Barnabas asked Matthew if he could talk to him.

"I really like what you do, so much so that I mentioned this to one of my former college instructors, and he thought it would be a good idea if I asked you if I could work as your assistant. That is, if you have "that" position available," said Barnabas, nervously.

Matthew was flattered. He had been in the organization since its inception and he did not have an assistant and no one had ever asked him this question before, perhaps because his work was so demanding and required a lot of overtime.

"As a matter of fact, I have been thinking about finding someone to help me out a little more. Let me get back with you," said Matthew.

A week went by before Matthew contacted Barnabas and told him that he liked his resume and that he was going to make plans to have him transferred into his division to work as his assistant.

Barnabas was ecstatic. He had only been with the company a short while, and now he was going to be an assistant to Matthew, the legend.

Matthew, an expert at his craft, was excited to have someone who wanted to learn and follow in his footsteps. Barnabas spent a lot of time with his new mentor, watching his every move and learning everything he could from the venerable leader. He accompanied Matthew on every business trip, and to every meeting and conference. The two sat side by side on airline trips. For his part, Matthew loved to hear Barnabas' tales of the organization's latest gossip and rumors.

Although Matthew and Barnabas never socialized together outside of the office, the two became inseparable inside the company. Matthew began to confide in Barnabas and quickly considered him a friend. It became a running joke to those who saw them together that whenever Matthew stood up, Barnabas stood up. Whenever Matthew sat down, Barnabas sat down.

Matthew had a funny and intellectual sense of humor. He often regaled employees with stories and jokes about events and people, past and present. The staff laughed heartily at the tales, and Barnabas laughed right along with them.

Matthew also had an insatiable work ethic. He was known to put in long hours at the office. He usually arrived at work before 7:00 a.m. and did not return home until 8:00 p.m. on most evenings. He frequently ate at his desk and rarely took vacations or did anything to get away from his vocation.

After years of keeping this grueling schedule, it began to take a toll on Matthew's health. He was having trouble sleeping at night and keeping food in his stomach, and he had frequent dizzy spells. His doctor diagnosed him with high blood pressure and exhaustion. Matthew began missing work on a regular basis, taking sick days. At times, he was so exhausted that he could not get out of bed in the morning. In Matthew's absence from work, Barnabas began managing the department and all decisions went through him—key phone calls, memos, and projects. When Matthew knew he wasn't going to be in the office, he also asked Barnabas to lead the weekly department meetings.

Barnabas developed relationships with key employees, taking them out to lunch and just sitting around bantering whenever time permitted. He allowed the employees to come and go as they pleased, saying he would cover for them if need be.

Barnabas also began cultivating relationships with Matthew's boss. Whenever he was in his presence, Barnabas made a point to speak to him. Once, when Matthew's boss asked Barnabas how things were going, Barnabas responded that he was busy because Matthew was away from the office, and he, Barnabas, was having to pick up the slack. Pretty soon, Matthew's boss began to confide in Barnabas more and more.

When Matthew was at work, and he ran the division meetings, Barnabas sat at the opposite end of the conference table and laughed and joked with a few of the employees while Matthew was talking. Matthew never said a word but it was obvious to some employees that it was disrespectful.

Barnabas was a sociable person, unlike Matthew. After work, Barnabas loved to frequent the local nightclubs and bars and he would invite employees to go along with him. One night after a few beers, Barnabas was overheard by a couple of employees saying he could run the division a lot better than Matthew.

Soon, Matthew's mental exhaustion began to take more of a physical toll on his body. Upon seeing his doctor, he was told to go home and get some rest. When things did not get better, Matthew was placed in the hospital for a full week.

When he was dismissed from the hospital, Matthew's doctor recommended that he take additional time off work and just get away from it all. A friend of Matthew's offered him the use of his cabin in the mountains, so Matthew, along with his wife, went on a three-week vacation.

Just prior to being admitted to the hospital, Matthew had offered a special projects position to Harrison, an employee in the division. The project was going to help the leadership team immensely. Harrison was thrilled and accepted the position on the spot.

Not long after Matthew left for vacation, Barnabas ran into Harrison in the break room.

"I heard you were going to accept the new special projects position," said Barnabas.

"Yep, it's a great opportunity. I can't wait to get started," said an excited Harrison.

"It's a dead-end position. I hope you realize that," said Barnabas with a look that spoke 'I know something you don't.'

"What do you mean it is a dead-end position? I was offered it by Matthew, the director of this whole division," said Harrison.

"Yeah, you were. But how long do you expect Matthew to be the boss? Haven't you heard? He's sick. He's been out of work because of mental exhaustion. You know what that means?" said Barnabas with a smirk on his face.

Harrison was puzzled. He did not know how to respond. Barnabas could see it on his face, so he continued.

"Look, if I were you, I'd stay put. There are going to be some changes in this division. You don't want to accept a position and then have the new boss think twice about it and do away with the whole thing, do you?" asked Barnabas.

When Matthew's three-week vacation was over, he returned to work refreshed and energized. Besides, he was coming back with a lighter load. The special projects position that he had given to Harrison would eliminate, along with the help of Barnabas, a lot on his plate.

Matthew felt it was time for him to meet with his staff, so he sent out an email detailing the importance of a 2:00 p.m. meeting the next afternoon. The general rule had been that if an employee had an outside appointment with a client during a called meeting, his or her absence was excused. However, for this meeting, everyone was expected to attend.

Not long after sending out the correspondence, Matthew had a visitor. It was Harrison. He told Matthew he had second thoughts and that he was not going to accept the new job. Matthew was taken aback.

"Why don't you want the position?" asked Matthew.

"Well, after you left for vacation, I had time to think about it, and I just don't believe the job is the right fit for me," said Harrison.

Matthew could have assigned the special projects position to Harrison anyway, but that was not his style. His philosophy had always been that if an employee wanted a position, he or she would put forth more effort and would enjoy the process, as well.

Later that afternoon, Barnabas ran into a couple of employees in the break room.

"I see on the schedule that you guys are having a client meeting tomorrow," he said.

"We were but we rescheduled because Matthew's email said everyone was supposed attend the meeting," one of them said.

"Oh, it's ok. Don't worry about it. I'll talk to Matthew. Besides, if I recall, your meeting will determine your quotas for the month," said Barnabas in a convincing but no-big-deal manner.

"Wow! That would be great. You're the best," said one of the employees as they walked away.

Matthew walked into the conference room the next afternoon and took his seat at the head of the table. As he surveyed the room, he noticed there were several empty seats.

"Where is everyone?" he asked.

No one said a word. Not even Barnabas, who sat at the end of the table opposite Matthew.

"Well, let's get started," said Matthew.

As he began the meeting, there were whispers at the other end of the table. Barnabas was carrying on a conversation with one of the employees. They were not loud but their voices were audible.

Matthew never said a word to Barnabas about his behavior. He continued with the meeting.

Matthew had always looked forward to having lunch in the company's cafeteria. That was a time for him to connect with his peers—the other division directors. There was always light banter as they told stories of the past or simply discussed the business issues of the day. But this time when he went into the cafeteria, his peers were nowhere to be found.

On the other hand, Barnabas began scheduling his lunch before or after Matthew ate his. He no longer spent as much time with

Matthew as he had in the past. They used to lunch together at least three to four times a week. One day, Matthew walked into the cafeteria, got his lunch, and strolled to his usual table. Shortly thereafter, Barnabas walked in with two of Matthew's peers. They got their lunch and sat at the other end of the cafeteria. Barnabas never looked Matthew's way.

Matthew began feeling isolated. His closest peers were no longer communicating with him, at least not on a regular basis. They were cordial but the closeness was gone. His jokes with his employees were no longer funny. Matthew had been back in the office for nearly two months, and his contact with Barnabas had been minimal.

Feeling sick again, Matthew started to miss days from work. However, this time his previously diagnosed physical exhaustion was worse. His high blood pressure was out of control, and he was now suffering from depression.

Barnabas, on the other hand, grew closer to Matthew's boss. He was now having lunch with him almost every day. More and more, Matthew's boss began to confide in Barnabas. Barnabas was also growing closer to Matthew's peers. When he was not visiting with them in their offices, they were playing Saturday morning golf.

It was not long before the higher-ups felt a change was needed. Matthew's boss, along with two of his peers, went to see him one day when he had called in sick. They did not beat around the bush. They told him he had been an integral part of the company's rise but they felt it would be best for him to resign.

Within days and after much heartache, Matthew did just that. He turned in his letter of resignation. There was no celebration or fanfare. Numerous employees did express their sadness. He did not have any ill feelings toward anyone in the organization.

Although his wife and children felt that Barnabas had betrayed him, Matthew never said an ill word about his long-time assistant.

For his efforts, Barnabas became the new head of the division and retired 15 years later after a successful career. During his tenure, the organization did not change much strategically. After all, he learned everything he knew from Matthew, a person many credited with keeping things afloat when the company went through its early lean years. Barnabas was successful in his new duties, growing the division's bottom line each year.

However, as time passed, many of the employees felt something was missing. Although the financials looked good, the workers complained about a certain deterioration in the division's culture. It lacked character.

Years later, a national news magazine featured a story on Matthew. In it, the reporter interviewed Barnabas. To his credit, Barnabas spoke glowingly about his former boss. "Everything that I know I learned from him," he was quoted as saying.

In the interview, however, Barnabas talked as if he had frequent contact with Matthew since he had left the company. But the truth was Barnabas had not spoken to him since the day Matthew left.

There are several lessons to be learned from Matthew's fate. First, Matthew did not take care of himself properly—physically or mentally. People with demanding jobs need to take the time to get away from the workplace. Matthew did not exercise or take vacations. As successful as he was, as he reached the top of his game, his tank began constantly running on empty.

Second, Matthew should have taken more time to vet Barnabas before he chose him as an assistant. Placing someone in a position of authority, in your absence, and not considering his or her character, will surely cause erosion in the relationship at some point, and it is akin to signing your own career death certificate.

Third, Matthew failed to discipline Barnabas when he was out of line. According to bestselling author Jim Hunter, when a human being enters a new environment, he will ask himself two subconscious questions: (1) How am I supposed to behave, and (2) What happens if I do not behave that way? Surely Barnabas was comfortable with his behavior because he was never held accountable for his misbehavior.

Finally, one would have thought Matthew's peers would have stepped in to help him during his time of need but they did not. Perhaps they, too, were jealous of Matthew's success. Conversely, Barnabas was a manipulator—pure and simple—with a huge ego. People like him will throw rocks and hide their hands and stop at nothing to get their way.

According to a study by Julianne Holt-Lunstad, a Brigham Young University professor, in the *Annals of Behavioral Medicine,* love-hate-relationships may negatively affect your blood pressure because these volatile and indecisive connections "don't help us deal with stress and are themselves a source of stress."

Holt-Lunstad says, "The type of friend we are talking about is someone we may really love or care about. However, they can also at times be unreliable, competitive, critical or frustrating. Most people have at least a few friends, family members or co-workers who fit the bill."

Based on contributions in this and prior research, Holt-Lunstad and her associates discovered that as many as half the people in anyone's sphere of influence would be classified as the type who could cause a person's blood pressure to rise. For those who cannot distance themselves from these kinds of friends, the next question is whether conflicted friendships could contribute to the development of cardiovascular problems such as clogged arteries.

In the leadership world, we have been conditioned to believe that the most important person in the organization is the leader. I do not accept this as a true assertion. The key person in the organization is the leader's chief assistant—the assistant principal, the assistant head coach, the assistant CEO. Leaders are hired to set the tone, the vision for the organization, and in doing so, they spend a lot of time away from the day-to-day operations of the business. This leaves the leader's second-in-command in place to run the company. The number two person is entrusted to carry out the leader's platform in his absence. No other single person, outside of the leader, can make or break the spirit of an organization more than the person who assumes the reins when the leader is away.

What about you?

1. Are the people in your sphere of influence worthy of being there?
2. Do you surround yourself with people who have your best interests at heart?
3. Do you surround yourself with wise men?
4. Can you trust your number two person?

REFLECTIONS

Chapter 6

Defining the Importance of Good Health

Several years ago, I walked into a co-worker's office to discuss a few administrative details. The conversation began with a little small talk. At one point, she asked me how I was doing. I said fine as long as my clothes do not keep falling off me. My co-worker then said, "Yeah, people have been wondering if you were okay because you've lost so much weight." People? What people? I began feeling self-conscious. I did not want anyone, for that matter, thinking that I was ill, because I was not! I immediately went to every office in the building to explain to my co-workers, the people I see every day, that I was losing weight on purpose.

I have struggled with obesity most of my life. There have been periods when I fought the weight battle and won, and there have been periods when I fought and lost. During my ninth grade year in high school, which was also my first year in the marching band, we spent the entire band camp outside in the hot Alabama heat. I lost about 20 pounds that August. During the summer heading into my senior year of high school, I lost 30 pounds and managed to keep most of it off for nearly four years. When I began working at Total System Service right out of college, I weighed 175 pounds. But as life got in the way, my weight began to creep up, pound by pound. For the next 18 years, I would become an expert yo-yo dieter.

Eating right and exercising pays dividends. I was in the best physical condition of my life in 2011-12.

Did you notice how I started this chapter talking about weight control? I love food. I find a good hamburger and hotdog hard to resist, and ribs and brownies have always been my favorites. That is why for most my life all I have ever wanted to do was lose weight. I did not think very much about being healthy. That type of mindset came to an end in my early forties when I woke up one morning and got on the bathroom scale. It read 279 pounds. Whoa! I could not believe it. In the throes of having a career that I was so passionate about, I had let myself go. I was no longer just overweight. I was severely obese and borderline ill. I knew right then and there that I had to do something, and fast.

The first thing I had to do was educate myself on the importance of good health. I started researching online how to eat smarter. There is a wealth of information available about how and what to eat. Whenever I feel the slightest bit ill, I immediately take inventory of foods I have been eating. I try to eat lean turkey, grilled or baked fish and grilled or baked chicken with no added salt, because most foods, whether in restaurants or grocery stores, already contain excessive sodium. I also try to stay away from cakes, cookies, and pies. Do I ever let my guard down? Of course I do. Every now and then I will eat something that I probably should not have, but the key to eating right is consistency of habit.

Since the early 1990s, I have been presenting the speech *Define Your Destiny*. I also wrote a chapter on this topic in my first book, *Stand Tall*. I have been telling people for years that if you want to achieve greatness you must have desire, positive relationships, goals, and a vision. However, there was one quality I left out—good health. In truth, you can have all the dreams and ambition in the world but if you do not take care of your body, your goals and vision will become moot points. Your health is the most important aspect of your being. I missed the boat on this for years. From a spiritual perspective, when I attend church, I hear people say all the time, "I want my salvation. I want my salvation. All I want is my salvation." Well, I am here to tell you, if you do not take care of your body, your salvation is going to come a lot quicker than you think.

Eating healthy includes various foods from each of the food groups, eaten proportionally in relation to your sex, age, weight and other factors such as pregnancy and your overall health condition.

Most Americans live their life in the red zone—meaning we are some busy people. Americans work an average of 46 hours a week, so where do we find the time to go home after work and cook a healthy meal? For most of us, having time to do such things is a luxury.[9]

I love walking around Moon Lake in Phenix City. It's my gym of choice.

In 2010, the federal government released the Dietary Guidelines for Americans in which its research showed that one-third of children and two-thirds of American adults exceed a healthy weight. Miriam E. Nelson, PhD, director of the John Hancock Research Center on Physical Activity at Tufts University, says, "The data clearly document that America is experiencing a public health crisis involving overweight and obesity...Primary prevention of obesity, starting in pregnancy and early childhood, is the single best

---

[9] Jessica Lietz, "The Importance of Practicing Good Health," *AZ Central,* http://healthyliving.azcentral.com/importance-practicing-good-health-1506.html

strategy for combating and reversing America's obesity epidemic for current and future generations."[10]

Nelson, who is one of the foremost activists of exercise in America and was the vice-chair of the Physical Activity Guidelines for Americans in 2008, also says, "Increased physical activity, while important, in and of itself will not solve our obesity problem."[9]

I do not like to exercise but physical activity is essential to being in good health. Studies by the U.S. Department of Health and Human Services suggest that the lack of exercise contributes to an increased risk of heart disease, diabetes and stroke; and the likelihood of your experiencing accidental injuries and the shortening of your lifespan.

Discovering good health is different for everyone but its importance cannot be overstated, and it has not been an easy process for me. I had to learn the hard way that being health conscious manifests itself in every area of my life. It is not just about eating right or exercising, although that is a major part of it. It is about having a holistic approach to life—the physical, mental, and spiritual needs being met all contribute to my well-being.

What about you?

1. Do you exercise regularly?
2. Do you eat right?
3. Do you see your doctor annually?

---

[10] "Guidelines to Good Health," *Tufts University Health & Nutrition Letter 29, no. 3 (2011),* http://search.proquest.com/docview/884214902?accountid=10275

REFLECTIONS

CHAPTER 7

DEFINING FORGIVENESS

Researchers who study forgiveness and its effects on our overall well-being are precise in how they define the term. Forgiveness is a change in one person's emotional outlook for being mistreated or harmed by another. The man feeling wronged no longer wants to exact revenge on the other individual. In some cases, it may even be a feeling of "good will" on the part of the forgiving one—i.e., I am doing you a favor by forgiving you. The act, in and of itself, is his willingness to accept the grief of being hurt and admit the suffering that comes with it.

On the other hand, researches are also clear about what forgiveness is not. It is not reconciliation, which means that both people, the one doing the wrong and the one who feels the wrongdoing, are willingly working together. It also does not mean forgetting. We have all heard the phrase, "forgive and forget." When a person forgets the bad deed, there is also the possibility of denial, and that denotes that the issue is still unresolved. Forgiveness is not excusing the pain but is taking the time to honor the feeling.[11]

The man or woman with an unforgiving spirit—anger, bitterness, revenge—will take this behavior into every relationship or experience they have unless the issue is resolved. I knew a man who had the philosophy, "Don't get mad, get even," and he taught this misbehavior to his children. One child took it to heart and it nearly ruined their family.

Forgiveness is a dedicated choice. Pardoning someone you feel has dealt you a bad hand requires vulnerability. If you don't decide to absolve them, those past feelings will continue to resurface. Getting immersed in the facts of the situation, understanding that there are two sides to every story, can help alleviate some of the pain, and may allow you to gain greater knowledge of how the situation is affecting your life.

The unforgiving person has no power. The control belongs in the hands of the one you feel betrayed you. Release the negative energy he has over you, because if you do not, you are allowing yourself to be defined by the pain.

It is hard to make another individual change. They may be oblivious to the need to or deny that there is actually a problem. So, what should you do? I think my grandmother said it best: "Just make sure you do the right thing." In the end, the only person you can transform is you. Perhaps it is you who needs it. If this is the case and you realize it after much reflection, do not be so hard on yourself. If you are really sorry for what you have done, come to

---

[11] "Understanding forgiveness, " *PBS.org*, http://www.pbs.org/thisemotional-life/topic/forgiveness/understanding-forgiveness

grips with it, sincerely admit it to the other person, and pray that they forgive you.

In order to feel the full effects of forgiveness, you must allow yourself to feel the pain and suffering of the person who wronged you. This feeling must be organic and not forced. According to Dr. Judith Orloff, in her book *The Power of Forgiveness: Why Revenge Doesn't Work*, "Some people, wanting to be 'spiritual' have prematurely tried to forgive."

"Turning the other cheek" is hard, especially when you feel they got away with something and you are too helpless to do anything about it. You just have to know that in the end the truth will come out and if you want to get them back, do not get mad and get even: get successful and happy knowing that you did not stoop to their level.[12]

Several years ago, I had a boss I felt did not want me working for him. My distrust of him came after the first conversation we had regarding my joining his department. He had just returned home from a European vacation. He called to tell me he was glad I was going to be in his department and to celebrate the occasion he brought me and the rest of the staff a bottle of wine from Paris. It was a kind gesture. I was excited. He never brought the subject up again, and I never saw the wine.

The following conversation may seem hard to believe but it is entirely true.

My boss had his secretary keep tabs on me. One day, as I was leaving the office, I told her I was going to meet a prospective client

---

[12] Judith Orloff, "The Power of Forgiveness: Why Revenge Doesn't Work," *Psychology Today, (2011),* http://www.psychologytoday.com/blog/emotional-freedom/201109/the-power-forgiveness-even-911

across town. I had not been in my car 10 minutes when my cell phone rang. It was the secretary.

"Where are you? What are you doing?" she asked suspiciously.

"I'm headed to the meeting I told you about," I said.

I drove across town for my conference. However, as soon as I pulled into the prospective client's parking lot, my cell phone rang again.

"Where are you? What are you doing?" she again asked with a hint of I-do-not-believe-you in her voice.

"I just arrived at the meeting that I told you about," I said, trying not to sound bothered.

Five minutes later, my meeting had begun when my cell phone rang again. I tried to ignore it but the prospective client nodded his approval for me to answer it, so I did.

"Where are you? What are you doing?" she asked.

"I'm in that meeting I told you about," I said trying not to look exasperated in front of my host.

My meeting continued, and ten minutes later my phone rang again. I was not going to answer it but the client said it was ok.

"Where are you? What are you doing?" she asked.

"I'm in a meeting," I said.

This time when I hung up the phone, the client looked at me in disbelief and said, "Is it that bad?"

"Yes, it is," I said, feeling as low as a worker could under those circumstances.

All of this and other issues within the office caused me to have an unforgiving and mistrusting attitude toward my supervisor. I really enjoyed the work I was doing but the environment was toxic, and I did not like being mistreated.

My perspective on forgiveness changed one day when I went to a conference and heard a speaker from Rwanda talk about the genocide in his native country.

The gentleman asked us to imagine waking up the next morning and our whole family was gone. In fact, he said to imagine our entire neighborhood was no longer there—no friends, no relatives, no grocery stores, not even the milkman. That is what happened to him. He was the only person left alive. The gentleman said he could have lived a life filled with rage and anger, but he chose not to. He then looked out at the audience and pointed at himself and then back to the audience and said, "If I can forgive, so can you." It was another one of the freeze-framed moments of my life. His message was so strong that I was overwhelmed with emotion. It was at that moment that I began to contemplate the importance of forgiveness, but the actual application of the act did not take place right away.

I carried the burden of unforgiveness with me for several more years. Long after I had left his department, I would see my former boss around town, and either I snarled at him or went out of my way to avoid him. One day, I received an email along with five other people, including my former boss. We were being invited to participate on a committee. I could have easily declined the invite but it was too great an opportunity to serve the community. As a result, I said yes, and he did, too. We ended up serving together.

The night before our first meeting I decided I was going to do it—I was going to apologize to him for my behavior toward him.

Even though I felt he had mistreated me when I was his employee, there was still no reason for me to behave in a likewise manner.

When I arrived for the committee meeting, he was already there. During one of the breaks, I asked him if we could talk. He said yes.

"I would like to apologize to you. For years I have held a lot of resentment toward you. It is not right. I am sorry. I hope you will forgive me," I said with relief.

"Well, I knew something was wrong. I could tell that you were upset with me about something," he said, sounding somewhat nervous as he spoke. We actually had a nice talk. He forgave me. We shook hands, and went back to the meeting.

Our conversation was liberating. It felt like the whole world had been lifted off of my shoulders. Since that encounter, whenever I see him, I no longer have those harsh feelings.

However, something interesting happened to our relationship that took it to another level. Not long after I had come to peace with my former boss, I was asked to speak at a local church. Like I do on so many occasions, I decided to visit the congregation three weeks before the scheduled program.

I arrived at the place of worship and took a seat in the back row. I had a good view of everyone in the congregation. Five rows in front of me I noticed my former boss and his wife. I was surprised. I did not know they attended that church.

At the end of the service, the pastor asked everyone in the congregation to come to the altar, so she could pray for us. As I exited the pew and made my way down the aisle, my former boss and his wife did the same, and I ended up walking right behind them.

As I stood at the altar, the pastor said a few words but what happened next was so surreal. She asked the congregation to "hold hands with the person standing next to you." Somehow my former boss and I were standing side by side. He looked at me and I looked at him (another one of those freeze-framed moments). We held hands. It was at that moment that I looked up (to God) with a wry smile and whispered to myself, "You think you're pretty funny, don't you?"

When someone you love and trust hurts you, there is a strong sense of betrayal, and quite possibly anger. Your every thought and internal conversation is about him or her. That is why holding a grudge can seem so rational.

Just being in the vicinity of the other person is not easy. It can be downright stressful. In the beginning, you might have to decide whether or not to attend events or gatherings where the two of you may come into contact with one another. There are two ways to handle this situation. First, know what triggers you. You must analyze your own emotions to know what it is about this person makes you so upset. Second, plan your response, as the Prevention Relationship Enhancement Program, or PREP, suggests. Ask yourself: What will I say if he says this? How will I handle it if he does that? If you enter into the situation of being in the presence of the person who wronged you with the proper mindset, it will help you move forward.

I know numerous people who have been deeply hurt by someone else. Depending on the degree of pain, the agony, the unhappiness, and the suffering can linger for years if not decades. I also know people who, because they have been wronged, have a vengeful spirit. They do not realize it is easier to forgive than carry around the emotional baggage of seeking retaliation on another individual. When I have forgiven someone, my other relationships were the beneficiaries. It freed me from spending my spare time bombarding my other friends and family with my negative (and not to mention "woe is me") attitude. I can attend church and listen to the sermon with a clear conscience. But when I'm in an unforgiving mindset, I do not hear anything. I feel better with a spirit of forgiveness.

What about you?

1. Is there someone in your life you need to forgive? If so, what will it take for you to take that step?

REFLECTIONS

Summary

Define Your Destiny is based on two parts of my life's journey. One is servant leadership. I first heard the term in the 1990s when Bill Turner stood on the stage at a Synovus employee meeting at the Columbus Convention and Trade Center and extolled the virtues of the world's oldest leadership philosophy, saying it would one day change the world. I firmly believe it can. However, in order for this change to take place in organizations, it will require a tremendous amount of consciousness on the part of their leaders so servant leadership does not become just another flavor-of-the-month.

The other part of my journey is self-awareness. I have been on this path my whole life but I didn't know what it was. The realization came to me in 2005 when I joined the staff of the Pastoral Institute, where deeply spiritual and philosophical conversations with my co-workers Fran, Ron, Stephen, and John were my favorite pastime. No group of people has made me think more of my life's purpose, reaching my higher self, and being one with God, than these four individuals.

Everyone has a story. *Define Your Destiny* is mine. I hope it and the accompanying lessons appeal to you. My life experiences, inside as well as outside of the classroom, have shaped who I am. Of course, I am sure genes have a role to play in there somewhere. I have tried to learn something from every endeavor I have undertaken, particularly as an adult. One of the basic premises of this text is the importance of awareness—of yourself and your surroundings.

If you are observant, the laboratory of life is never ending.

In other words, now is the time to go out and *Define Your Destiny*

REFERENCES

Burrus, Daniel. "Think Big… and Then Think Bigger." *Huffington Post*, Apr. 3, 2013. http://www.huffingtonpost.com/daniel-burrus/think-bigand-then-think-b_b_3007689.html

Flora, Carlin. The Mix Bag Buddy and Other Friendship Conundrums. *Psychology Today, 2013.* http://www.psychologytoday.com/articles/201212/the-mixed-bag-buddy-and-other-friendship-conundrums

"Guidelines to Good Health." *Tufts University Health & Nutrition Letter 29, no. 3 (2011).* http://search.proquest.com/docview/884214902?accountid=10275

Hill, Napoleon. *Think and Grow Rich.* New York: Fawcett Crest, 1960.

Lietz, Jessica. "The Importance of Practicing Good Health." *AZ Central,* n.d. http://healthyliving.azcentral.com/importance-practicing-good-health-1506.html

McKay, Brett and Kate McKay. "How and Why to Become a Lifelong Learner." *Art of Manliness* (blog). Mar.18, 2013. http://www.artofmanliness.com/2013/03/18/how-and-why-to-become-a-lifelong-learner/

Orloff, Judith. The Power of Forgiveness: Why Revenge Doesn't Work. *Psychology Today, 2011.* http://www.psychologytoday.com/blog/emotional-freedom/201109/the-power-forgiveness-even-911

Rutledge, Pamela. Want to Keep Your Job? Get More Education. *Psychology Today,* 2009. http://www.psychologytoday.com/blog/positively-media/200911/want-keep-your-job-get-more-education

Ryan, John. The Three Fundamentals of Leadership. *Forbes,* April 29, 2009. http://www.forbes.com/2009/04/29/vision-communication-judgment-leadership-managing-ccl.html.

Smith, Julia. "The Growing Importance of Education in the Job Market." *Value of Education* (blog). Mar. 21, 2013. http://blog.online.colostate.edu/blog/value-of-education/growing-importance-of-education-in-the-job-market/

Sword, Rosemary. Kindness is the Key. *Psychology Today,* 2013. http://www.psychologytoday.com/blog/the-time-cure/201307/kindness-is-the-key

"Understanding forgiveness." *PBS.org. n.d.* http://www.pbs.org/thisemotionallife/topic/forgiveness/understanding-forgiveness

About the Author

Kelvin A. Redd is the director of the Center for Servant Leadership, a division of the Pastoral Institute in Columbus, Georgia. For more than twenty-five years, he has made the study of what makes great people great his life's calling.

Redd spent thirteen years in key positions at Synovus Financial Corp., which was *Fortune Magazine*'s "Best Place to Work in America" in 1999. He is the author of *Stand Tall: Essays on Life and Servant Leadership* and publisher of the blog iLead2Serve. A rising leadership strategist and twenty-first-century thought leader, he travels the country providing keynote speeches and workshops on servant leadership and self-awareness.

Redd earned a BA in history from Auburn University and an MS in management, with a concentration in leadership and organizational effectiveness, from Troy University.

Resources

For more information on servant leadership, please visit:

My Personal Blog
http://www.iLead2Serve.com

The Center for Servant Leadership, a division of the Pastoral Institute
http://www.pilink.org/plaintext/servantbrleadership/servant-brleadership.aspx

Twitter
@KelvinRedd

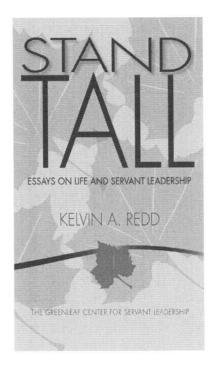

"Kelvin Redd and I share the belief that servant leadership can transform our world. His wonderful collection *Stand Tall: Essays on Life and Servant Leadership*, illuminates the path on the journey of becoming a servant leader. His clear focus on the practical aspects of this journey is a great and useful guide for our fellow travelers."

-Jack Lowe, Chairman of the Board, TDIndustries

"Kelvin has done a masterful job of writing essays that will guide you in both grasping and applying the principles of Servant Leadership into your life. The best part for me is that Kelvin is the "real deal," i.e., he truly believes and lives out these principles on a daily basis in his own life."

-Jim Hunter, Author of *The World's Most Powerful Leadership Principle*

"By blending important thoughts and writings of others into his observations and personal experiences, Kelvin Redd provides a guidebook for a life of servant leadership. His conclusion that servant leadership is a journey, not a destination, makes clear that our goal must be to reflect servant leadership ideals each day along the way, not to "become" a servant leader. Kelvin's method of applying these precious principles to daily life illustrates how the awareness and practice of servant leadership in one's life can change relationships and, most importantly, lives.

-Frank D. Brown, President Emeritus, Columbus State University

16214165R00060

Made in the USA
San Bernardino, CA
23 October 2014